LAND

of the

ESKIMAUX'S or LABRADOR

Hudson Straits

Bellisle

GULF
of
ST. LAURENCE

NEW
FOUNDLAND

St LAURENCE

C.

St John

C. Breton

Sable I.

Gt BANK
of Newfoundland

NOVA SCOTIA

NEW ENGLAND

NEW
HAMPSHIRE

Bay of Fundy

NEW YORK

MASSACHUSETS

CONNECTICUT

Cape Cod

St Georges Bank

Long I.

Nantucket I.

2½ Minutes

3 Minutes

NEW JERSEY

Philadel.ᵃ

Delaware
Bay

3 Minutes

Chesapeak
Bay

3 Minutes

C. Hatteras

3 Minutes

ATLANTIC OCEAN

Bermuda I.

A
CHART
of The
GULF STREAM

James Poupard, sculp.

Part of BARARY

Spain

Portugal

France

B. Biscay

Iceland

NORWAY

Baltick
Sea

MEDITER: SEAN

Benjamin Franklin

Benjamin Franklin

Inventor, Statesman, and Patriot

by R. Conrad Stein

RAND McNALLY & COMPANY CHICAGO • NEW YORK • SAN FRANCISCO

Line drawings, and color illustrations on the front cover and on pages 19 and 46 by William Jacobson

Library of Congress Cataloging in Publication Data

Stein, R   Conrad.
   Benjamin Franklin: inventor, statesman, and patriot.
   SUMMARY: A biography of the printer, inventor, and statesman who played an influential role in the early history of the United States.
   1. Franklin, Benjamin, 1706–1790–Juvenile literature. [1. Franklin, Benjamin, 1706–1790. 2. Statesmen, American. 3. United States—History—Colonial period—Biography] I. Jacobson, William, illus. II. Title.
E302.6.F8S875   973.3'2'0924 [B] [92]   72-3884
ISBN 0-528-82478-3
ISBN 0-528-82479-1 (lib. bdg.)

PRECEDING PAGES:
Conference of the Treaty of Peace with England
By Benjamin West
HENRY FRANCIS DU PONT WINTERTHUR MUSEUM

ENDSHEET MAP: Courtesy of the Library of Congress

Contents

Introduction

This is a story of the life of one of the most amazing men in American history. Benjamin Franklin was a printer, an inventor, a writer, a scientist, a diplomat, and a statesman. It could be said that Ben was a jack-of-all-trades—and a master of most of them.

In the period of history known as the Renaissance, men such as Michelangelo and Leonardo da Vinci became famous not only as artists but also as engineers, architects, inventors, and scientists. The term *Renaissance man* has since been used to describe people who have a genius, not just in one special area, but in broad areas of human knowledge. Franklin can truly be thought of as America's Renaissance man.

As a boy in Boston young Ben was inventive and imaginative. He constantly tried to find more efficient means to accomplish his ends. To help him catch fish more easily, he built a pier; to aid him in swimming, he devised an early version of hand fins.

His experience with school was brief. Ben went only two years to a grammar school, and he failed arithmetic.

He became an independent printer at the age of twenty-two when he opened a printshop in Philadelphia. He published a newspaper and later published *Poor Richard's Almanack*. The *Almanack* was an interesting and often hilarious pamphlet that became popular throughout the world.

At the age of forty-two Ben retired from business and devoted his life to science and invention. He was the first to prove that lightning was really electricity, and he was the first to use the terms *positive* and *negative* in connection with electricity. His many inventions included a new type stove and the first bifocal eyeglasses.

Franklin's success as a diplomat was phenomenal. He managed to persuade the French to aid the American colonies in their fight against England. It could be said that Franklin went to Paris and won the Revolutionary War. After the war he helped to write the Constitution of the new United States of America.

Franklin died at the age of eighty-four. Years before his death he wrote to his mother that he hoped people would say of him, "He lived usefully," rather than, "He died rich." He did not die rich, but he certainly lived one of the most useful and interesting lives of any American in all history.

R. CONRAD STEIN

CHAPTER ONE

A Boy from Boston

A group of boys splashed around in a pond in Boston during the summer of 1716. One boy, a ten-year-old, had been flying a kite earlier that morning. Now he looked at his kite and then looked back at his friends swimming in the pond. "I'm going to try something," he thought.

He grabbed the kite and ran, holding it above his head. The kite jerked a few times and finally soared in the wind.

"Watch this!" the boy shouted to his friends.

He let out more string, sending the kite higher. Then he stepped backward toward the pond. His friends, interested now, stood in the shallow water and watched.

The boy guided the string so that the kite flew behind him. He waded backward into the water. When he was into the pond up to his waist, he lay on his back and kicked. He held the string to his chest and kicked again. The string pulled tight, and the force of the wind pushing the kite pulled the boy to the middle of the pond.

"Just like a ship," he yelled. "This is how a ship works."

One of the boys stood on the bank, shaking his head.

"That Ben Franklin," he said. "He's always trying something new."

And Benjamin Franklin was constantly trying out new ideas when he was a boy. Once he showed up at the pond with a pair of paddles, which he had carved out of wood. He tried to get more power from his swimming stroke by holding the paddles in his hands and using them to propel himself through the water.

Young Ben Franklin must have spent each night dreaming of ideas he wanted to try out and then spent all day putting them to work.

One summer Ben and his friends thought they had discovered a new way to catch fish. Fish were often trapped in shallow ponds near the Boston Harbor after the tide went out. The boys found they could splash around in the ponds and scoop up fish with their hands, but when the cool autumn weather came over Boston, this method of fishing became impractical. So they looked to their leader to figure out a way to catch the fish without getting their feet wet.

"We'll build a pier," Ben said. "We'll build it right out to the middle of the pond, so we can walk out on it and bring the fish in with sticks."

"Good idea," the boys responded. And they all agreed that Ben should be the architect, the engineer, and the construction boss.

This was the biggest project in Ben's life. Building a pier was the kind of thing he had always dreamed about.

Ben and his friends found a load of bricks stacked neatly near the pond.

"This will be perfect," said Ben. "Let's get them over to the pond."

"But Ben," one of the boys said. "Don't you think that someone might own these bricks?"

"No, we can use them," Ben answered.

The boys brought the bricks one by one to the pond. There Ben and another boy began the painstaking task of laying the bricks alongside each other to form a pier. Ben worked on his knees with his arms elbow deep in the cold water. When he could no longer kneel and do the job, he jumped into the water and continued putting the bricks in place.

It was almost dark when Ben and his friends finished. They had built a sturdy and even a beautiful pier. A full-grown man could ride a horse to the end of it, and not one brick would fall off. Ben thought the pier would last at least a hundred years.

The boys stood on the end of the pier and pulled in fish with sticks, just as Ben told them they would.

"Hey! What did you boys do with these bricks?" a man shouted.

Ben turned. The man appeared to be a construction worker, and he was with a gang of four or five other workers.

"We built a pier so we could catch fish," Ben answered.

"And you never thought that these bricks were put here so we could build a house, did you?"

"No," said Ben after a pause.

The man leaned back and shook with laughter. The other workers had a good laugh also. Finally the leader of the work gang stopped laughing.

"Now you listen to me," he said. "I want you boys to take all of those bricks out of the water and put them right back where you found them. Do you understand?"

"Yes," Ben said slowly.

"Now!" the man shouted.

"Yes sir," Ben snapped.

All the bricks that Ben had laid so carefully were taken up and returned to the pile. His pier, built to last a hundred years, was gone before it was one day old.

Ben worked feverishly on each of his new projects. He hated anything that took him away from the model boat he might be building or from the fort he was constructing in the woods.

Ben's neighbors would probably have considered such activities foolish, for the Boston of his boyhood was a deeply religious city. The most important man in town was a stern minister named Cotton Mather, who each Sunday frightened his congregation with sermons that warned of hellfire and damnation. Every Bostonian spent much of his time in Mather's church. Ben believed in God, but he thought that constant prayer and long hours in church were a waste of time. He would rather be out building something.

One day Ben was helping his mother salt meat so it could be stored for the winter.

"Mother," Ben said, "perhaps we should pray over this meat."

His mother was startled. Young Ben had never shown this much enthusiasm about religion before.

"Certainly we should pray over the meat," she answered. "I'm so glad you thought about it."

Ben and his mother bowed their heads and said the traditional prayer.

"Good," Ben said at the conclusion of the prayer. "Now that we've blessed the whole batch of meat we won't have to say Grace before each meal."

His mother shook her head in a gesture of hopelessness. She knew that Ben Franklin would never become a clergyman as she and her husband had hoped he would.

Ben was the fifteenth born of seventeen children. His father, Josiah Franklin, was a poor but hardworking candlemaker. Ben was born in a modest house on Milk Street in Boston on January 17, 1706. Even when Ben was very young, Josiah knew that his son was the smartest of the family.

"This boy is going into the clergy," Josiah declared.

Benjamin was put into a grammar school when he was eight years old. At that age all his other brothers were put to work at trades.

Ben loved to read, and it came easily to him. Ben once wrote that he could not remember a time in his life when he was not able to read.

He also displayed an early talent for writing and wrote themes with such force and clarity that his instructors could hardly believe they were written by a ten-year-old boy.

But Ben had no success at all with arithmetic. He failed that subject miserably and even dreaded attending classes because he could not cope with long arithmetic problems.

It was probably Ben's realistic mind that caused his downfall in arithmetic. Much of the learning in those days was done by repetition, which meant endless hours of reciting multiplication tables and the like. This, to Ben, was a waste of time. He often had to use some complicated mathematics to work on one of his projects, and when he could use arithmetic in such a practical way, he had no difficulties at all. He did, however, have a terrible time trying to memorize six times seven, six times eight, six times nine . . . .

Gradually Josiah Franklin realized that his son was not cut out for the clergy. His difficulties in arithmetic and his tendency to fall asleep during church services convinced the elder Franklin that Ben would never become a minister.

Josiah took Ben out of school after only two years. Ben was put to work in his father's shop, helping to make candles and running around Boston to deliver them. This work did not suit Ben either, and he had a desire to run off to sea as one of his older brothers had done years earlier.

One day he mentioned his intention to go to sea to his father.

"I will not allow another son of mine to become a sailor," Josiah shouted. "It's a wicked life. We'll find a trade for you on the land where you belong."

Josiah had to find a trade for Ben in a hurry. He took Ben on long walks through the city to observe tradesmen at work. They looked at the work of bricklayers, carpenters, and bakers. Ben enjoyed these walks with his father, and he was especially interested in the tools used by the tradesmen. But he still had a burning desire to board a ship and sail the seas.

Many months passed before Josiah discovered the proper trade for his son. He finally decided that Ben should become an apprentice printer. Josiah thought it would be a perfect trade for him and one that would keep him on land.

There were also two other reasons for Josiah's decision. First, he knew that Ben loved books, so printing ought to be agreeable to his son since it would put him in contact with new books. Second, Ben's brother James had just set up a small printing shop at the corner of Queen Street and Dasset Alley in Boston. Ben could easily serve as an apprentice to his brother, and he would gradually lose his inclination to go to sea. This solution was so obvious that Josiah wondered why he had not thought of it earlier.

When Ben was twelve years old, he signed the papers to become an apprentice printer in his brother's shop. In those days signing an apprenticeship contract was the same as signing oneself into slavery. Ben could be jailed if he tried to break the contract by running away to sea. His contract compelled him to work for his brother for the next nine years. James Franklin was to provide him with room and board, but he was to collect no wages until his last year as an apprentice, when he would be twenty-one years old.

After Ben signed the contract, Josiah Franklin breathed a sigh of relief. His son had been saved from entering the wicked world of a sailor.

Ben learned the printing trade quickly. It was a trade he would practice for the next thirty years.

One of his jobs was to operate the printing press. It was a monotonous task, one that was not at all challenging for his curious mind. The operator had to place sheets of paper, one by one, over the type. Then he had to turn a wooden handle that was connected to a screw shaft, which then put pressure on the plate, and the printing was "pressed" to the paper. This simple operation took a strong back and little imagination.

Typesetting was a different matter. A typesetter worked on a bench called a stone. To set type properly, letters and spaces had to be fitted precisely into a plate, and corrections had to be made with tiny wooden shims. It was a painstaking job, but Ben found it challenging. Typesetting was a skill—something one could practice, learn, and finally master. Gradually Ben became the best typesetter in the shop, better even than his brother James.

Conflict had developed early between the two brothers. James was twenty-one years old when Ben signed on as his apprentice. James expected all apprentices to do their work and keep their mouths shut, but Ben did not act that way at all. Instead he eagerly made suggestions about how to run the shop with greater efficiency. Most of Ben's

suggestions were good, but James still refused to listen to opinions voiced by a mere apprentice. In some cases, however, James would scoff at one of Ben's new ideas one day but quietly put the idea into practice the next.

Sometimes their fighting was ugly. James was an ambitious, hot-tempered young man. Any reversal in his business upset him, and he often took out his anger on his younger brother. Often Ben was slapped and kicked for no apparent reason. There was no way that twelve-year-old Ben could retaliate, because his contract bound him to his brother's shop for the next nine years.

Ben, unhappy and confused, often turned to his father for advice.

"James is a young man, and you're just a boy," Josiah Franklin would explain. "James is bound to lose his temper now and then."

"But I work hard in the shop," Ben protested. "And I know what I'm doing on the stone and on the press and in everything else."

"Ben," Josiah said softly. "Why don't you just try keeping your opinions to yourself in the shop."

"But when I see an easier way to do something, what could be wrong with my telling James about it?"

"James wants to be the boss in his own shop," Josiah said. "I know because I was the same way when I was his age."

Ben followed his father's advice. Although he found it frustrating to put up with work methods that he thought were backward, he stopped disagreeing with James. Instead Ben kept his ideas stored in his mind. He was developing a dream—a distant dream, but a possibility nevertheless. Perhaps someday he would open his own shop.

The situation in James's shop, while not happy, at least became livable. Ben did his work and kept his mouth shut, but he needed to talk over his troubles with someone. He grew to depend on his father's wisdom and experience. The two developed a deep friendship that lasted many years.

When Ben was not working, he was in his room reading. He read anything he could get his hands on. He read the book *Pilgrim's Progress* and enjoyed it. He was also fond of classical books such as Plutarch's *Lives*. When Ben was sixteen, he read a book, written by an author named Tryon, that recommended a vegetable diet. Franklin thought he would try this diet, and he became a vegetarian for a year. The diet helped him to buy more books. Since Ben did not receive wages, James had been paying a local boardinghouse to provide him with room and board. When Ben went on his vegetable diet, he convinced James to give the boarding money directly to him. He found he could live on half of what James paid the boardinghouse, and he used the remaining money for books.

Besides reading, Ben tried his hand at writing. When he was only thirteen, he wrote a poem about a Boston lighthouse keeper and his family who had died during a storm. Ben's uncle read the poem and encouraged him to print it and try to sell copies. The poem sold rather well in the streets of Boston, and Ben was feeling proud of himself until he showed a copy to his father.

"My God, Ben! This is terrible stuff!" Josiah exclaimed.

"But I sold a lot of copies of it," Ben said.

"That only goes to show that people in this town will buy anything," Josiah answered.

Years later, when Franklin wrote his *Autobiography*, he called his first poems "wretched stuff," and he thanked his father for saving him from becoming a very bad poet. Finally Ben's attention turned to prose and letter writing. In the years to come he would be hailed as America's greatest writer.

In 1721 James Franklin had begun to print a newspaper called the *New England Courant*, one of the first newspapers published in the British colonies. The paper featured letters that were sent in by people in the Boston community. Ben wanted desperately to submit some of his own writing to the *Courant*, but he knew his brother would punish him if he even suggested the idea.

One day, when he was sixteen, Ben disguised his handwriting and wrote a letter, which he slipped under the door of the *Courant* office. In the letter he described himself as a widow woman who wanted to express "her" views on the problems of the Boston community. Thus he created a fictitious character whom he called Silence Dogood. She was supposed to be a wise, middle-aged woman who had experienced many hardships and was fond of giving advice. She promised to send a new letter to the *Courant* every fortnight.

Ben's first letter described the birth and early childhood of Mrs. Dogood. It also showed something about young Ben's imagination. He wrote: "At the time of my birth, my parents were on ship-board. . . . My entrance into this troublesome world was attended with the death of my father . . . for as he, poor man, stood upon the deck rejoicing at my

birth, a merciless wave entered the ship, and in one moment carried him beyond reprieve."

In all, Ben wrote fourteen Silence Dogood articles. They dealt with Mrs. Dogood's opinions on such subjects as religion, drunkenness, local poetry, and old maids. After the first few articles had appeared, Silence Dogood became the talk of Boston.

One day at the shop Ben overheard a discussion between his brother and a friend.

"What do you make of this Silence Dogood?" the friend asked.

"She's sensational," James said. "She has a marvelous sense of humor. I'm selling papers as fast as I can print them since she started writing."

"Did you hear that Cotton Mather quoted her in his last sermon?"

"I heard about that," said James. "I wish that woman would come to the shop someday. I would like to meet her."

Ben was working on the stone when he heard the conversation.

He tried to hold back but could not. He burst out laughing so hard that everyone in the shop stared at him.

With the help of Mrs. Dogood's contributions, the *Courant* became a popular newspaper. But James Franklin had had confidence in the success of his newspaper from the beginning. Shortly after he started publishing, he even thought he could challenge Cotton Mather.

In 1721 Boston had been hit by an epidemic of smallpox. Vaccine to combat this disease existed, but little was known about the mysterious process called inoculation. Cotton Mather had read about the process, and he urged in a sermon that all citizens of Boston be inoculated.

When James heard of Mather's plans, he stormed in the printshop.

"That old man Mather does not know what he's talking about," James shouted to one of his friends. "No one knows anything about what inoculation can do to people."

Ben had remained silent for a long time, but on this issue he had to disagree.

"Inoculation has worked in other cities," Ben said. "We've got to try something, or the smallpox will spread over the whole city."

James looked down sternly at his brother.

"Since when have you ever agreed with Cotton Mather?" he asked.

"Usually I don't, but I read a report on inoculation, and I think we should try it in Boston."

"You just keep quiet and get back to work," James said.

James turned back to his friend.

"Imagine trying to cure someone of a disease by giving him a case of it. What's wrong with that Mather anyway?"

Ben quietly resumed his work, but he was shaking with anger.

Inoculation was tried in Boston with great success, but the issue opened up a feud between James Franklin and Cotton Mather. One day, in 1722, an article that was critical of the government appeared in the *Courant*. Mather used his influence to persuade the provincial council of Boston to send James Franklin to jail because of the article in his paper.

Ben was furious about his brother's arrest. Although he often disagreed with James, he was still shocked that the government had the power to throw someone in jail for merely expressing his opinion.

While James was in jail, Ben kept the newspaper operating. He wrote another Silence Dogood article that reflected his anger about

James's arrest. He wrote: "Without freedom of thought there can be no such thing as wisdom; and no such thing as public liberty without freedom of speech."

Some fifty years later the spirit of writing such as this would spark the American Revolution.

Despite Ben's protest his brother remained in jail for thirty days. After he was released, he was forbidden to operate a newspaper in the city of Boston by order of the provincial council. James Franklin had tangled with Cotton Mather, and he had lost. But by this time Ben had joined the fight also. He was determined to keep the *Courant* circulating on the streets of Boston despite Mather's wishes.

Ben, James, and Josiah Franklin got together and secretly revised Ben's apprenticeship papers. Ben became the acting publisher of the *Courant*, while James remained the manager. There was no court order against Ben Franklin publishing a newspaper, and the *Courant* continued to be a popular paper.

James's time in jail made him bitter and intensified his hot temper. Again he took his anger out on his younger brother, but Ben, at seventeen, was less inclined to take his brother's abuse without fighting back. The situation was not helped by James learning that Ben was the celebrated Silence Dogood. There were times when Josiah Franklin had to break up fistfights between his two sons.

Ben decided he had had enough and began to make plans to run away. This would mean breaking his apprenticeship contract, which could put him in jail. But the court order prohibiting James from operating a newspaper worked in Ben's favor. Ben was now the publisher of the *Courant*, and although he was still technically an apprentice, he knew that James would never take the revised contract into court. There was a great deal of shady wording in that contract, and a court could find that James was in more trouble than his runaway younger brother.

Ben did not care where he went as long as it was away from Boston. The best way to get out of the city was by ship, but he knew that a ship's captain would suspect he was a runaway apprentice and therefore refuse him passage. So he devised a plan to get himself on a ship. In his *Autobiography* he wrote about this plan: "My friend Collins ... agreed with the captain of a New York sloop for my passage, under the notion of my being a young acquaintance of his, that had got a naughty girl with child, whose family would compel me to marry her." The captain felt sorry for Ben and agreed to take him to New York.

One night seventeen-year-old Ben quietly packed a chest loaded with his books and a few clothes. He sneaked out of Boston and boarded the ship bound for New York.

Franklin arrived in New York in September 1723 with no job and very little money. New York at the time was smaller than Boston. It was a strange-looking, garbled city built by the conservative Dutch. Ben was amazed when he discovered that there was not a bookstore in the entire town.

The first thing he needed was a job, so he went to the shop of the only printer in New York, an old man named William Bradford.

"I don't need any help now, young man," Mr. Bradford told Ben. "People in this town don't read much."

"I've discovered that," Ben answered.

"But my son owns a shop in Philadelphia," Bradford said. "I think he could use a good hand if you'd care to go there."

Ben thought for a moment.

"Very well," he said. "I guess I'll have to go to Philadelphia."

Ben arranged to have his chest shipped, and he started out on what would prove to be a very difficult trip to Philadelphia. The first ship he took ran into a storm and almost sank off Long Island. If Ben had any inclinations left about going to sea, they were probably discouraged during that dangerous voyage. His ship finally docked at Perth Amboy in New Jersey.

From Perth Amboy Ben wanted to go to any point on the Delaware River, where he hoped he could catch a boat to Philadelphia. Since he was running low on money, Ben figured the only way he could get to the Delaware was to walk. So he walked—fifty miles across the colony of New Jersey. He walked for two days, much of the time in rainy weather, until he reached the city of Burlington, on the Delaware. He had slept only a few hours at some inns along the road.

Early in the evening Ben found a sailboat that was leaving Burlington and heading down the Delaware to Philadelphia. He boarded the boat, hoping he could relax and catch up on some much-needed sleep. But luck was not with him that night. A few miles out of Burlington the wind died, and all the passengers were put to work rowing.

Ben and the others rowed through most of the night. When the boat finally docked at Philadelphia the next morning, Ben offered to pay for his passage, but the captain refused to accept payment because Ben had had to row the entire time he was on board. But Ben, though he had little money, insisted on paying. He later wrote that he wanted to pay because "a man [is] sometimes more generous when he has but a little money than when he has plenty, perhaps through fear of being thought to have but little."

Ben was a sad sight when he stumbled off the boat. He had worn the same clothes since he left Boston. Now they were shrunk from the storm off Long Island, and they were torn after his fifty-mile walk. He was weary after a night of constant rowing, and he was hungry. Not far from the dock Ben went into a bakery, where he hoped to buy some biscuits. Ben often ate biscuits for breakfast while he lived in Boston.

"May I have a few biscuits, please?" Ben asked the baker.

"Biscuits! We don't make them here," the man answered.

Travel was difficult in those days, and cities often developed different customs and totally different foodstuffs.

"Well, can I have a threepenny loaf then?" asked Ben.

Franklin with Loaf of Bread
By David Rent Etter
COURTESY INA CORPORATION

"I never heard of a threepenny loaf. Where are you from?"

"All right then," Ben said. "Please give me three pennies' worth of any kind of bread you have."

The baker gave him three huge loaves of bread. It was much more than three pennies could buy in Boston. Ben walked out of the shop munching one loaf and holding the other two under his arm.

Now, munching bread and wearing tattered clothing, Ben truly looked ridiculous as he walked down the streets, nervously looking left and right at the sights of his new city. Many Philadelphians stopped to stare at this odd-looking youngster. One young girl stood on her front step and laughed at the sight of him, which was particularly embarrassing for young Ben.

He ran into a woman whom he recognized as a fellow passenger with him on the boat the night before. Ben chatted with her for a moment and gave her the rest of his bread. He then found lodgings and slept the rest of the day and all through the night.

No one in Philadelphia that night knew they were gaining a new citizen. Franklin would remain a Philadelphian for the rest of his life. He was destined to become the most famous man in the history of that city.

CHAPTER TWO

A Successful Printer

Ben tidied himself up the best he could the next morning and took a brief walk around Philadelphia. Later in the day he would seek the shop of Andrew Bradford, where he hoped to find a job, but first he wanted to see a little more of his new city. He liked what he saw. Ben sensed that there was more excitement here than in sleepy little New York or in sternly religious Boston. He thought, that first morning, that here was a city where he could settle down and stay for a while.

When Ben arrived at Andrew Bradford's shop, he was surprised to find that old Mr. William Bradford was there.

"Good afternoon, Ben," William Bradford said. "I rode here from New York just the other day. I told my son about you."

Andrew Bradford introduced himself and said, "I wish you had arrived here a week ago, Ben. I had a job open, but I just hired a new man."

"Don't worry about a job, Ben," the elder Bradford said. "There's a new printer in town. I'll take you over and introduce you to him right now."

Ben and William Bradford walked to a run-down-looking shop owned by a Mr. Samuel Keimer.

"I could use a good man," Keimer told Ben. "Let's see how you set type."

Ben was shocked at the condition of the shop. It was dirty and disorganized and had pieces of paper and type plates scattered about. Ben wondered how Keimer could even find his type in such a mess. Still he managed to set a few lines.

"I can see you know what you're doing," Keimer said. "I'll hire you at journeyman's wages."

Franklin was pleased to be taken on as a journeyman right away, but when he started working, he found out why Keimer had been so generous. Keimer knew very little about printing. The shop had a dilapidated old press, which had not been used in some years. Ben spent many nights getting the press into shape. Gradually, through his energy, the place began to look like a printshop.

Ben adapted easily to Philadelphia life. He was an independent printer now and not just a mere apprentice who had to follow orders and keep his mouth shut.

He lodged with a family who lived near the printshop. One of the daughters of this family was a Miss Deborah Read. This was the same young girl who had laughed at Franklin when she saw him munching on bread as he walked down the street in his raggedy clothing. She was also the same girl Franklin would later marry.

One day Ben wrote a letter to one of his sisters' husbands, telling him how much he liked Philadelphia. By chance Sir William Keith, the governor of Pennsylvania, was traveling with Ben's brother-in-law and read the letter. The governor could hardly believe that such a well-written letter came from a boy of seventeen.

Weeks later Ben's employer, Samuel Keimer, was looking out the window while Ben worked on the press. Keimer dreamed a lot. There were two shops in Philadelphia, but there was hardly enough work for one. Still, Keimer hoped that someday he would become the largest printer in the city.

"Come over here, Ben," Keimer called. "Look out the window for a moment."

Ben crowded up to the window with his employer.

"That man over there." Keimer pointed. "Have you ever seen him before?"

"No, I don't think so," Ben said.

"If I'm not mistaken, that man is William Keith, the governor of Pennsylvania," Keimer said excitedly. "I wonder what he's doing around my shop?"

"Perhaps he has lost his way," Ben suggested.

"Look, Ben! He's coming this way," Keimer shouted.

Ben thought the man would faint from excitement.

"He's going to place an order," said Keimer. "Government printing! This will make me rich."

Ben quietly resumed his work. The governor walked in the front door.

"Is this the shop of Samuel Keimer?" he asked.

"It most certainly is," Keimer said delightedly.

"And does a Mr. Ben Franklin work here?"

"Yes, but . . . but . . ." said Keimer.

"Are you Ben Franklin?" the governor asked of the young man working on the press.

"Yes, I am," said Ben surprised.

"I met your brother-in-law a while ago, Ben, and I thought we might sup together today."

Ben agreed to the luncheon while Keimer, as Ben later wrote, "stared like a pig poisoned."

At lunch Governor Keith suggested that Ben start his own print-shop. The governor assured Ben that he would help give him a start by placing government printing orders at his shop.

"I'd love to have my own shop," Ben said. "But where would I ever get the money to start out?"

"Perhaps your father could loan it to you," the governor suggested.

Ben thought about it. He knew his father was better off now than he was when Ben had been a child. Perhaps his father would advance him the money. Anyway, it was worth a try. Ben shook hands with the governor and made preparations for his return to Boston.

When he arrived in Boston, he was afraid the old feud between him and his brother would start again, but it did not, although James did treat him coldly. However, the rest of Ben's family welcomed him with genuine joy. The only problem occurred when Ben brought up the business of a loan.

"I am not going to risk such a large amount of money on a business run by an eighteen-year-old," his father said.

Ben knew his father well enough to know that further discussion would be useless. Disappointed, he returned to Philadelphia and told Governor Keith about his father's refusal to grant the loan.

"Well, don't despair, Ben," Keith said. "You go ahead and book passage to London. I'll give you a letter of credit, and you can buy a press and anything else you may need."

"London . . . Letter of credit," Ben stammered. "But I can hardly believe all of this."

"Well, go on, boy. Get packing."

Ben was too surprised to say anything other than "thank you." He packed but had to wait several weeks before he could board a ship. While he waited, he wondered, "When will he give me that letter of credit? How good will it be when I get to London? Why did he not offer me the letter before suggesting I get the money from Father?"

Finally the governor's secretary told Ben to get on the ship and wait. The letter would be delivered before the ship sailed.

Ben did what he was told to do. He waited while the anchor was lifted, and he waited while the sails were unfurled and the ship slipped out to sea. The promised letter of credit was never delivered.

Ben got off the ship in London in much the same circumstances as when he had arrived in Philadelphia. He was penniless and lost. Governor Keith, it seemed, was a hopeless dreamer who made many promises but never saw them through. Later Franklin wrote about Keith: "He wish'd to please everybody; and, having little to give, he gave expectations."

Ben did not have too much to worry about though. He was at this time a master printer, and London was the printing center of the English-speaking world. He got immediate employment in a printshop owned by Samuel Palmer. Ben found London to be an exciting city. He had never seen so many bookstores in one place before. It was in London that Ben first became interested in studying foreign languages. Before he died, he had taught himself six languages.

Although London fascinated him, Ben wanted desperately to return to Philadelphia. The promises of William Keith had excited his imagination. Ben wanted to own his own printshop. After spending a year and a half in London, he returned home.

Once in Philadelphia Ben returned to work at Keimer's printshop. But he did not last long at his old job. He and Keimer had never gotten along well, and one day the two had a violent argument in the shop. Ben quit his job in disgust. Another young man, named Hugh Meredith, who had been working for Keimer, also walked out after the argument. Meredith was a hard worker, but he was a drunkard. He and Ben were good friends though, and Meredith's father was very much impressed with young Ben Franklin. The elder Meredith made Ben an offer.

"I want to set you and my son up in a shop, Ben. I think you are a good influence on my boy. I'll loan the two of you all the money you will need."

"You'll get the money back," Ben said. "You'll get it back with interest. I know I can be successful with a printshop."

Meredith loaned Franklin the money and also made him promise that he would try to get his son Hugh to stop drinking.

In 1728 Ben and his partner started a shop on Market Street. He was an independent businessman at the age of twenty-two. His was the third printshop operating in Philadelphia. One was owned by Keimer, and the other by Andrew Bradford. Competition among the three would be fierce.

OVERLEAF: *Benjamin Franklin, Printer*
By John Ward Dunsmore
THE NEW-YORK HISTORICAL SOCIETY

But Ben's plans were bold. Indeed he was ruthless when competing with his rivals for printing orders.

A group of Quakers had given Keimer a contract to print a book dealing with the history of the Quaker religion. Ben found out that Keimer had fallen behind the delivery date, and he told the Quakers that he could deliver the books faster. The Quakers took the order away from Keimer and placed it with Ben. He had to work day and night for weeks in order to deliver the books on time.

Government printing was the most profitable work available. When Ben opened his business, Andrew Bradford's shop was getting most of the printing orders. Ben saw the job Bradford had done on an address from the Pennsylvania Assembly to the governor. Franklin thought it was a poor job, so he reprinted the address correctly and in cleaner type, then distributed his copies to each member of the assembly. Soon afterward a few government printing orders found their way into Ben's shop.

In 1729 there was a money crisis in Pennsylvania. At the time all money was in gold or silver coins that were hoarded by a few wealthy people. Workers and debtors, like Franklin, had a difficult time getting enough money together to pay their bills. Except for the wealthy, most of the other people in the state wanted the state to issue paper money.

Franklin saw that if paper money were issued, it would help him in two ways. First, cheaper money would help get his shop out of debt, and second, he knew he would get the printing order as he was the only printer in the state who was skilled enough to design and print paper currency.

Ben wrote an essay called *A Modest Enquiry into the Nature and Necessity of a Paper Currency.* He printed this essay in pamphlet form and distributed it on the streets. His arguments for issuing paper money were so convincing that no one could hope to argue against him. Soon after he wrote the essay, the state decided to issue paper money, and Franklin's shop got the printing order.

Ben also believed in doing little things in order to secure new business. When he bought paper, he did not have it delivered. Instead he picked up the paper at the mill himself and pushed it down the street in a wheelbarrow. Thus he advertised himself: Here goes Ben Franklin, the hardest-working printer in Philadelphia.

Gradually Ben was able to make a profit at his shop, and he slowly paid off his debts. One commitment he was never able to fulfill was his promise to Hugh Meredith's father that he would get Hugh to give up drinking once they were in business together. Young Meredith continued to be a hard drinker, and Ben finally bought his half of the shop after the business was two years old. Hugh Meredith drifted out of town, and Ben never saw him again.

When Ben first opened his shop, he had one secret, burning ambition. He wanted to publish his own newspaper. At that time there was already one newspaper in town, the *American Weekly Mercury*, published by Andrew Bradford.

One day Ben foolishly told a friend of Samuel Keimer's that he intended to start a newspaper. When Keimer heard this, he rushed to publish a newspaper of his own. So before Ben even got started, there were two newspapers in Philadelphia. Again competition would be tough, but Ben had a distinct advantage. Although he was only twenty-four, Ben was already the best writer in America.

Ben's first job was to drive Keimer out of the newspaper business. He began by submitting articles to Keimer's rival paper, the *Mercury*. As he had done with the Silence Dogood series, Ben disguised his writing as that of a middle-aged woman. He signed his articles under the name of The Busy-Body. These articles were lively and funny stories that were especially written to the working people of the community.

Franklin knew what the people of Philadelphia wanted to read. After he started The Busy-Body series, everyone in the city bought the *Mercury*, and Keimer's paper was soon out of business. Keimer had put a lot of money in his newspaper, and he could never make up the loss. He finally had to sell his paper to Benjamin Franklin, the man whose writing had put it out of business. Keimer then left for the West Indies and was never seen in Philadelphia again. He also never found out that Franklin was "The Busy-Body" who had ruined his newspaper.

Franklin called his new paper *The Pennsylvania Gazette*. Under his guidance it became the most respected newspaper in America.

Not all of Franklin's efforts were immediate success stories. There was a large German-speaking community in the city when Ben started his newspaper. So in 1732 Ben published a paper, the *Philadelphische Zeitung*, aimed at the Germans. He put a lot of time and money into this paper, but it failed after only a few issues. Ben took his losses on the *Zeitung* and forgot about it. As he later wrote about failure: "To err is human, to repent divine, to persist devilish."

As Franklin pulled himself out of debt, he began to think more about marriage. He always had a special feeling for Deborah Read, the girl who had laughed at him when he first arrived in Philadelphia. Deborah, a handsome but not particularly pretty woman, was a great deal like Ben, strong and hardworking. They were both poor but ambitious people, with similar family backgrounds.

Ben and Deborah were married in September 1730. A short time later a son, William, was born. Soon the family grew to include their lovely daughter, Sarah, and another boy, Francis, who died of smallpox at the age of four.

The Franklins were not the most romantic young couple in Philadelphia. Rather they viewed their marriage as a partnership to better their lives and the lives of their children.

With Deborah's help the Franklin business expanded. A stationery store, which Deborah ran, was added to the printshop. In addition to stationery and books she sold coffee, tea, cheese, chocolate, and even a special medical salve that was made by her mother.

When Franklin first started his printshop, he organized a discussion group called the Junto. The club was mostly made up of young tradesmen who were trying to start their own businesses. Sometimes it was called "the Leather Apron Club" because so many of the members wore the leather aprons typical of tradesmen.

At first the members of the Junto discussed local business issues. But as more people joined the group, the topics broadened to national problems. They discussed slavery, which Franklin unequivocally opposed. He thought it dreadful that such a wicked institution was allowed to begin in the colonies in the first place. They discussed another controversial issue, the education of women. Franklin thought it was ridiculous that women did not receive an education beyond merely learning to read. On this issue he drew many arguments from some of the other young men of the Junto.

Members of the Junto eventually changed the cultural life of Philadelphia. In 1731 they formed the first circulating library in the colonies. Anyone could stop and read at the library, but only members could take books out. As the library grew, people from other cities spoke of Philadelphians as being the most well-read of any in the colonies. The library was Franklin's suggestion.

When Ben was twenty-six years old, he launched his most successful business venture. In 1732 he put together the first issue of *Poor*

Benjamin Franklin, the Fireman
By Charles Washington Wright

Richard's Almanack. In a few years he would sell these almanacs faster than his press could turn them out.

Almanacs were second only to the Bible in colonial homes. They were pocket-size books that contained information on practically everything. There was a great deal of astrology in the almanacs as well as recipes, calendars listing holidays, and poems, jokes, odd facts, and little maxims and phrases that were designed to amuse the hardworking colonists.

The almanac written by Poor Richard was similar to every other almanac being read at the time, except that Poor Richard was really Benjamin Franklin.

It was Franklin's wit, humor, and wisdom that made *Poor Richard's Almanack* an immediate success. The colonists roared at phrases such as these in *Poor Richard's Almanack:* "Fish and visitors smell in three days." "He's a fool that makes his doctor his heir." "Keep your eyes wide open before marriage, half shut afterwards." "Three may keep a secret if two of them are dead." "Tim was so learned that he could name a horse in nine languages; so ignorant that he bought a cow to ride on."

Most of these sayings were not Franklin's own. They came from many lands and different cultures. One old saying that has haunted American children for generations once appeared in Franklin's almanac: "Early to bed and early to rise makes a man healthy, wealthy, and wise."

Franklin used his almanac to speak out against his pet peeves. He hated blabbermouths, so he wrote: "The worst wheel of the cart makes the most noise." He wrote this advice to clergymen: "A good example is the best sermon." His advice on friendship: "The same man cannot be both friend and flatterer." His ideas on frugality: "Creditors have better memories than debtors."

A new issue of *Poor Richard's Almanack* came out every year. Each new issue was bought up as soon as it got to the bookstores. It was the best seller in the colonies and was also sold in England and on the Continent. The French especially were delighted with the almanac written by *Bonhomme Richard.*

Franklin's almanac and his newspaper made him the most widely read man in the colonies. He was offered positions in the government but was suspicious of them. As he once wrote in the almanac: "The first mistake in public business is the going into it." But he was becoming so well respected that he could hardly avoid taking some government appointments.

In 1736 he was made clerk of the Pennsylvania Assembly. In 1737 he became the postmaster of Philadelphia. He gave his city the most efficient post office in the colonies. Also, aided by members of the Junto, he formed the city's first fire department and first full-time police force.

In 1743 Franklin wrote an article urging Pennsylvania to form a university. Six years later the forerunner of the University of Pennsylvania was established, and Franklin was named its first president. He remained president of the university for the next seven years. This was quite an honor for a man who only had two years of formal education.

Franklin's almanac and newspaper had made him financially independent. He had helped several young men go into the printing business in other cities and was receiving a percentage of the profits of these shops. Through hard work and shrewd investing he had gathered together all the money he would ever need.

As Ben was able to relax his efforts at making money, he was able to devote more time to science and invention, his primary interests. He had been reading science books all his life and had been tinkering with inventions since the first time he had tried to swim with a pair of paddles in his hands.

In 1748, after thirty years of work, Franklin turned his shop over to his partner. He moved his family from busy Market Street to a house on quiet Race Street, where he could set up a laboratory, a small shop, and a private library. He left the business world to devote his energies exclusively to science.

If Franklin had decided to stay in business, he could easily have become a wealthy man. But he summed up his notions of life and wealth in a letter written to his mother in 1750. He wrote: "I would rather have it said 'He lived usefully' than 'He died rich.'"

At the age of forty-two Ben entered the third stage of his life. He had gone from apprentice to businessman and now to a life of science.

A fourth stage, Franklin the statesman, was yet to come. But when Franklin retired from business, the American Revolution was still some twenty-five years away. George Washington was just sixteen years old, Patrick Henry twelve, and Thomas Jefferson five.

CHAPTER THREE

A Man of Science and Invention

Franklin was interested most in the new and mysterious study of electricity. It had been known since ancient times that strange sparks could be produced by rubbing certain objects. These sparks were loosely called electricity. Little was known about how these sparks originated or how to control them.

In Franklin's time electricity was a curiosity. In fact, in the colonies, it was used as a sideshow act. Wandering magicians with gypsy-type wagons mystified the colonists with electrical tricks.

One day Franklin watched such a show. The "magician" was a performer named Dr. Spencer. He put on a spectacular show, making a young farm boy's hair stand on end while he pulled sparks from the frightened boy's nose and ears. The colonists watching the show were shocked and frightened by it all. Ben watched the act with interest, and afterward he spoke with Dr. Spencer.

"Very interesting act, Dr. Spencer," Ben said.

"Thank you, Mr. Franklin."

"Can you explain how these tricks work?" Franklin asked. "I've become interested in electricity of late, and I'm curious about much of your act."

"How the tricks work, Mr. Franklin?" Spencer said surprised. "Now

I couldn't do that. I just do the same things over and over again, and they always work."

This discussion did not satisfy Ben at all. He bought all of Spencer's equipment on the spot and moved it to his new house on Race Street. With these props from a sideshow act, Franklin began his study of electricity.

Franklin's new interest became a passion with him. He wrote to a friend: "I never was before engaged in any study that so totally engrossed my attention." When Franklin devoted himself in such a way toward a subject, things were bound to happen.

One piece of equipment that Franklin used often was a primitive electric condenser called a Leyden jar. This was a jar, wrapped with foil and filled with water, that had been developed by scientists working in the Dutch city of Leyden. Electricity could be generated, usually by rubbing a glass tube, and then stored in the Leyden jar for later use.

Franklin was not satisfied with the simple Leyden jar he was using, so he developed a better one. He hooked thirty small Leyden jars together and found that he could store much more electricity in his new device. He later made a still more improved condenser by hooking glass and lead plates together. He called this new condenser an electric battery. It was indeed a battery, and it was the world's first.

Since little was known about electricity, Franklin, without knowing it, performed many dangerous experiments. In one experiment he almost electrocuted himself. He thought, wrongly, that the meat of an animal would be more tender if the animal were killed by an electric shock rather than by conventional means. With this theory in mind he tried to kill a turkey by electrocuting it with a current from a powerful Leyden jar. Franklin tried to hold the bird between his feet and apply the electrodes to its wings. The turkey, of course, had other ideas. The turkey squirmed from Ben's grasp, and the electrodes slipped into his hands. He wrote what happened next: "I then felt what I know not well how to describe: a universal blow throughout my whole body from head to foot."

Franklin was shaken up by the experience, but he survived. It would seem that he would have learned to be cautious after receiving such a jolt, but he was not. He performed many other dangerous experiments. He said about his attempt to kill the turkey by electricity: "I meant to kill a turkey, and instead, almost killed a goose."

He once proposed an electrical picnic. He suggested that everyone interested in electricity should gather in a Philadelphia park to eat chicken that had been roasted on an electrical fire and to be entertained by watching cannons being fired electrically. For after-dinner drinks Franklin suggested a smashing electrical cocktail. His idea was to serve wine in a thin glass that had been charged with electricity and that "when brought to the lips, gives a shock if the party be close shaved."

In 1752 Franklin wrote about what became his most famous experiment. Up to Franklin's time people regarded lightning as a strange and evil force. Stone Age men shivered in caves while lightning bolts cracked outside. Men of Franklin's time were almost as ignorant and as fearful of lightning as men of the Stone Age.

Franklin believed that lightning was really electricity. He thought that those terrifying flashes in the sky were actually gigantic electrical sparks. They were frightfully powerful sparks, but they had exactly the same properties as the sparks he could create in his laboratory. And, he thought, lightning could be controlled in the same ways he controlled his laboratory sparks.

In an earlier experiment Franklin had learned that electricity is attracted more easily to a pointed object than it is to a blunt one. Since he thought that lightning was electricity, he concluded that if he could get a pointed rod high enough into a thundercloud, the lightning would be drawn off toward the rod.

At first he suggested that such a rod be placed at the top of a church steeple, but since there was no steeple high enough for him to prove his theory, he later hit on the idea of a kite. He wrote: "As soon as any of the thunder-clouds come over the kite, the pointed wire will draw the electric fire from them, and the kite, with all the twine . . . will stand out in every way, and be attracted by an approaching finger."

Again this was a terribly dangerous experiment. No one is absolutely sure whether or not Franklin actually performed it. Fifteen years after Franklin proposed the kite experiment, an English scientist named Joseph Priestley wrote that Franklin did perform the experiment and that his son, William, assisted him with the kite. Since Franklin had read Priestley's account and did not disagree with it, we can assume that Franklin and his son flew a kite into a thundercloud and observed lightning drawn to the pointed rod attached to the kite.

Franklin's extraordinary good luck continued during this kite experiment, the most dangerous of all his experiments. While performing this experiment, he was lucky he was not killed.

The kite experiment led to his discovery of the lightning rod. A lightning rod is a pointed rod attached to the top of a building or the mast of a ship, with a wire leading either to the ground or the sea. Lightning bolts that used to destroy buildings were instead drawn to the lightning rod and then dispersed harmlessly into the ground.

No one knows how many lives were saved by the discovery of the lightning rod. They are still found on houses and barns in farm areas throughout the world. For years after their discovery they were called Franklin rods.

In 1751 Franklin had performed an experiment that was less spectacular than his lightning experiments but probably more important. He described how a man who has a normal amount of electricity within him can, by rubbing a glass tube, transfer some of his electricity into the tube. This man now has less than a normal amount of electricity

within him, and he is said to be charged *negatively*. If a second man touches the tube, he will pick up the electricity that was once with the first man. The second man will then have more than a normal amount of electricity, and he is said to be charged *positively*. Thus Franklin was the first to use the terms *positive* and *negative* in connection with electricity. His discovery would revolutionize the study of electricity forever.

When Ben was not experimenting with electricity, he was tinkering with inventions. While he was still a busy printer, Franklin had designed a new stove for his home. The old fireplaces were smoky and terribly inefficient. Franklin's new stove could be placed in the middle of a room. It had an air box that worked like a radiator, heating the air and circulating it throughout the room. Other people built the new stove, known as the Franklin stove, from his design, and it soon replaced fireplaces in America and England.

There are many other Franklin inventions. He designed a meter that could be connected to the axle of a cart and would show the number of miles the cart had traveled. When he was old and losing his sight, Franklin designed a pair of bifocal eyeglasses. The bottom half of these eyeglasses helped him to read; the top half helped him to see distances. He built a chair with a writing table attached to the arm. Every schoolchild knows what this chair looks like.

Franklin never tried to patent any one of his inventions. The lightning rod and Franklin stove alone could have made him rich if he had attempted to make a profit from these devices. Instead he shared his ideas freely with the world. He wrote: "As we enjoy great advantages from the inventions of others, we should be glad of an opportunity to serve others by an invention of ours; and this we should do freely and generously."

Franklin became interested in scientific farming and bought a farm in nearby Burlington, New Jersey. He discovered that plaster of Paris was an excellent fertilizer but had trouble convincing the neighboring farmers of his findings. One autumn he painted plaster of Paris on his field in large white letters spelling out "THIS FIELD HAS BEEN PLASTERED." The fall rains washed the plaster of Paris away, but the next spring the letters appeared again in grass that was far lusher and greener than the rest of the field.

He once designed a musical instrument called an armonica, which was played by touching the fingers to rotating glass. This instrument became popular in Germany, and composers no less than Beethoven and Mozart wrote music for Franklin's armonica. Franklin loved music. In addition to the armonica he played the violin, harp, and guitar. Also he was a good singer.

Franklin's work became known to scientists throughout the world. He had written articles on such subjects as geology, meteorology, mathematics, physics, medicine, chemistry, navigation, and astronomy. His work was widely read in European universities. He received honorary degrees from Harvard, Yale, William and Mary, and Oxford. He was elected to the Royal Society of London, and he received a letter of commendation from the king of France. Franklin was recognized as one of the world's leading scientists. All this from a man who had gone but two years to grammar school and who had failed arithmetic.

For ten years Ben worked, undisturbed, as a scientist, inventor, and man of letters. These were easily the happiest years of his life. If it had been possible, Ben would have continued experimenting, inventing, and producing work that would benefit all of mankind. But it was not to happen, for his country was in trouble. There were Indian wars on the frontier, and there were nagging problems with England. The troubled colonists needed help, so they turned to Ben Franklin, their wisest man.

There is no doubt that the people of the colonies needed Franklin. No other man was to contribute more to the American Revolution and the start of a new nation. But it seems a shame that he had to be pulled away from scientific inquiry after only ten years. His accomplishments were so many in those ten years that now we can only dream about what miracles were left unperformed by this amazing man of science.

CHAPTER FOUR

A General, a Diplomat, and a Statesman

In the 1700s war raged almost constantly in Europe. These wars between old European rivals often spilled over to the New World. The British and French colonists had little interest in the European wars, but they were often caught in the middle.

Such was the case in 1747 when England was at war with France and Spain. In July of that year French and Spanish privateers attacked two plantations in New Castle, Delaware, just a few miles from Philadelphia. Fear spread through the city that Philadelphia would be the next target of the ships. The city assembly was dominated by Quakers, who refused to vote money for arms, even for self-defense.

Franklin published a pamphlet called *Plain Truth*, in which he painted a grim picture of what would happen if the privateers attacked defenseless Philadephia. In the pamphlet he warned that the city would be sacked and burned, and many innocent people would be slaughtered. *Plain Truth* was probably an exaggerated account, but it worked. It scared even the Quakers, who finally voted the money, and a militia of 10,000 men was formed.

Franklin organized the defenders but declined an offer to be a colonel of the militia because he had had no previous military experience. Instead he served as a common soldier.

49

OVERLEAF: *Franklin Before the Privy Council*
By Christian Schussele
HENRY E. HUNTINGTON LIBRARY AND ART GALLERY

Philadelphians felt safer with the militia on guard, but Franklin believed the city needed cannons to bolster its defenses. In 1748 he went to New York to try to persuade Governor George Clinton to lend some of New York's cannons to Philadelphia. At first the governor flatly refused to part with any of his cannons. But at dinner Franklin, noticing the governor's fondness for wine, thought he had found a way to get Governor Clinton to change his mind.

"Let's drink a toast to New York," Franklin urged.

"A good idea," agreed the governor.

Franklin proposed more toasts (called bumpers in those days). The two men drank to every city on the eastern seaboard that Franklin could think of. Soon the governor was mellow enough to promise Franklin six cannons. They continued drinking, and as Franklin later wrote: "After a few more bumpers he advanced to ten; and at length he very good-naturedly conceded eighteen."

Franklin disliked military life, but he was forced to serve once more. In 1752 war broke out again between England and France, and the colonies once more were caught in the middle. The French enlisted the aid of several Indian tribes and encouraged them to attack colonial towns in what later became known as the French and Indian wars.

In 1755 a group of Shawnees attacked a small village called Gnadenhuetten, which was just seventy-five miles from Philadelphia. Again the frightened Philadelphians called on Franklin for help, and he led a small force to the outlying settlements of Pennsylvania, where he recruited volunteers and supervised the building of forts. In western Pennsylvania he was called General Franklin.

As Franklin organized the defense of Pennsylvania, he was also urging the different colonies to unite and provide for a common defense. He was one of the first to advocate such a union, but his proposal did not get very far. First, England was opposed to a union among the colonies. The mother country feared that if the colonies were united, they might decide on a course of independence. Second, individual colonies were reluctant to form a union. Each colony jealously guarded its own independence and was suspicious of the proposed union. Franklin's arguments for union were, as usual, sound, but it would be many years before the idea would be accepted in the American colonies.

In 1753 Franklin became the deputy postmaster for all the colonies. His new position required him to travel often. More and more he began to think of the colonies as a whole. In Franklin's mind, at least, the colonies were a united country.

In 1757 Franklin sailed to London on a mission for the Pennsylvania Assembly. Years earlier Pennsylvania had been founded by the Quaker William Penn. Penn's intentions were that the colony should be a land of religious freedom and peace among Europeans and Indians. But when William Penn died, his noble ideas died with him.

Now his sons, Thomas and Richard Penn, sat in England growing wealthy on the vast landholdings that once belonged to their father. The Penns refused to pay taxes on their land even though every small farmer in the colony was taxed. Franklin's job was to persuade the Penns to pay taxes.

Franklin's son, William, journeyed with him to London. He wanted to take the whole family, but Sally (Sarah) was in school, and Deborah was afraid of an ocean crossing. The trip to London took just thirty days. At the age of fifty-one Franklin returned to a city he had not seen in thirty-three years.

Negotiating with the Penns proved to be impossible. The stubborn brothers refused to listen to Franklin's arguments about taxes. Franklin often left the discussions shaking his head and muttering curses about the arrogant Penn brothers.

Franklin stayed in London for the next five years, acting as an unofficial representative of the colonies. He made friends among members of the British Parliament and urged them to pass legislation that would start helping the colonists instead of hindering them. He also met many British scientists with whom he had been corresponding for many years.

He returned to Philadelphia in 1762 but was sent back to London just two years later, this time to present a petition to the British crown. This was to be a routine visit, and before he left, he told Deborah that he would return in just a few months. Franklin had no idea that he would not see his home again for more than ten years.

The British government was caught in a money crisis when Franklin returned to London. Lord Grenville, the chief adviser to King George III, proposed a harsh tax on certain items, such as legal papers, that were sold in the colonies. The act creating the tax was called the Stamp Act. It was the most hated tax ever imposed in America.

The Stamp Act was a purely political move. The British people were already heavily taxed, and there would be bitter complaints in Parlia-

OVERLEAF: *The Declaration of Independence*
By John Trumbull
YALE UNIVERSITY ART GALLERY

ment if more taxes were imposed on them. Since the colonists had no representatives in Parliament, Lord Grenville thought it would be safer to tax them. Soon after the passage of the Stamp Act the cry "taxation without representation" was heard in America. This act, probably a major cause of the Revolution, caused riots in every one of the colonies. Agents appointed to collect the tax were beaten up and shot at. The colonists refused to buy any British-made goods.

Franklin was opposed to the tax, but his opposition was not vigorous enough to please the American people. Franklin had preferred to work quietly with his friends in Parliament for repeal of the act. The colonists viewed Franklin's tactics as his acceptance of the tax. For the first time in his life he had misjudged the temper of his countrymen.

All over the colonies Franklin was denounced as a traitor. There was even a rumor that he had accepted a bribe to be silent during passage of the Stamp Act. In Philadelphia there were threats to attack the Franklin home and burn it down. Deborah heard about the threats but refused to leave her house. Instead she got help from some of her friends and waited for the attackers in her front room with a rifle on her lap. Luckily, the home was never attacked.

In 1766 Parliament had second thoughts about the Stamp Act. A hearing was called, and Franklin, who was ill with the gout, was called to testify. For three hours Franklin answered questions about the act. His arguments for repeal were so persuasive that the act was dropped just a few weeks after the hearing. When word of repeal reached America, Franklin was again toasted as a hero.

For the next nine years Franklin remained in London trying to iron out the differences between the colonies and the mother country, but the Stamp Act had left scars that would never heal. Each year the differences between England and the colonies grew. In England King George III stubbornly refused to grant representation to the colonists. In America groups such as the Sons of Liberty, led by Patrick Henry and Samuel Adams, urged revolution and independence regardless of what the king might do.

Franklin patiently tried to deal with both sides. After the Boston Tea Party he even offered to pay for the tea dumped in the Boston Harbor if Parliament would repeal the tax on tea. Parliament refused.

Despite his efforts the situation grew worse. Franklin knew that a revolution in the colonies was near and that war would almost certainly follow. He had been loyal to the king all his life, but now he would aid the colonies in their fight against England.

In 1775 Franklin returned home knowing that there was no chance remaining for peace between England and her colonies. While he was still at sea, American and British troops fought a brief battle at Lexington and Concord, Massachusetts, where some one hundred men were killed. A bitter Revolutionary War had begun.

Franklin was sixty-nine when he returned to Philadelphia. It was a depressing arrival. His wife, Deborah, whom he had missed so much while in London, had died the year before. His son, William, now the governor of New Jersey, was his political enemy. William was a loyal Tory and refused to fight against the British flag. Even after the war Franklin and his son would never again be on friendly terms. These family problems added to his grief about the war that was being fought in his land. It was a war he had tried so hard to prevent.

Franklin knew that hard work was the best way to combat unhappiness. The day after he returned to Philadelphia, he became a delegate to the Continental Congress. In 1776 he read Thomas Jefferson's first draft of the Declaration of Independence. Jefferson's original version read: "We hold these truths to be sacred and undeniable that all men are created equal." Franklin crossed out "sacred and undeniable" and wrote instead "self-evident." He thought that the feeling would be stronger that way, and of course, he was right.

The Declaration of Independence was prepared while war was actually being fought between England and the colonies. The men who signed the document were criminals in the eyes of the British. If they were captured, they would be hung as traitors. A famous story goes that when John Hancock signed the Declaration, he said, "We must all hang together." Franklin, so the story continues, added, "Yes, we must indeed all hang together, or most assuredly we shall all hang separately."

The story of the Revolutionary War is one of the most interesting chapters in all history. It seemed that the weak colonists would have no chance at all in a war against mighty Britain, but the United States was blessed with its most brilliant leaders during a time when she needed them most. It took the genius of men such as Washington, Jefferson, Adams, and Franklin to win a war and start a new nation.

But the Americans also needed the help of another country. There was no way they could win the war alone. They looked to France, Bri-

OVERLEAF: *Battle of Bennington Prisoners*
By Leroy Williams
BENNINGTON MUSEUM, BENNINGTON, VERMONT;
FORWARD COLOR PRODUCTIONS, INC.

tain's oldest rival in Europe. It would be an enormous job to persuade the French to join the rebellious Americans in what looked to be a hopeless war. In 1776 they sent their most able diplomat to Paris—seventy-year-old Benjamin Franklin.

Franklin's reception in Paris was sensational. Even he had no idea how popular he would be among the French people. His *Poor Richard's Almanack* and a later book, *The Way to Wealth*, had been read by Frenchmen for years. His electrical experiments also excited the science-loving French. But even more it was his wit, wisdom, and folksiness that made him an immediate success with the French.

The French thought that all Americans were backwoodsmen. While this was certainly not the case with Franklin, he let the image grow anyway. "Give the people what they want to see," he thought. So he walked the streets of Paris wearing plain brown clothes with a fur hat perched on his head. He even wore this hat when he mingled with upper-class Parisians, who wore the traditional white wigs. No party given in Paris was successful without his presence.

To the man on the street Franklin was more of a hero than the king of France. Huge crowds followed him wherever he went. His face appeared on portraits, watches, bracelets, and even on snuffboxes. He wrote his daughter, Sally, that all these trinkets "have made your father's face as well known as that of the moon."

Franklin did everything he could to keep his popularity at a high level. He would need all the support he could get for the job ahead.

For the first year he was in France, Franklin could do nothing to persuade King Louis XVI to support America in its war with England. Finally in December 1777 word arrived in Paris that a British army had been defeated in a battle at Saratoga, New York. After Saratoga the king of France agreed to sign an alliance with the United States, but only if Spain signed also. This was discouraging news. Franklin knew that Spain would be even more reluctant than France to help the Americans.

Not willing to wait for Spain to sign an alliance, Franklin tried a bold move. There was an unsuspecting British spy in Paris named Paul Wentworth. Franklin called Wentworth for what was supposed to be a secret meeting, but he knew that French spies were watching Wentworth's every move.

Wentworth was a confused man after he left the meeting with Franklin. The two had talked for hours, but it seemed that Franklin had said nothing. Wentworth had no idea he was being used. French spies found out about the meeting as Franklin knew they would. A rumor was immediately circulated that America was ready to make peace with England and that the two countries then intended to attack French colonies in the West Indies. The rumor was entirely false, but Franklin did nothing to discourage it. It was precisely what he wanted to happen. Soon after the meeting the frightened French king signed a treaty with the Americans without waiting for Spain.

In one masterful move Franklin influenced a major power to join in the war against England. His work in Paris would bring victory to his country. Few other diplomats in all history had been as successful as the seventy-two-year-old American.

The treaty meant that war existed between France and Great Britain. Later Spain and Holland joined the war, and a host of smaller countries became hostile toward England. Suddenly England found that almost all of Europe was against her. And it all started with a treaty that a retired printer had secured with the king of France.

With pressure from her European enemies and military reversals in North America, England could not continue the war being fought in the New World. She was forced to make peace with her former colonies. The Americans had won an impossible victory—a victory they could never have won without Benjamin Franklin.

Other Americans, including John Jay and John Adams, were sent abroad to draft the peace treaty, but it was Franklin who did most of the work. There was much disagreement among the Americans. Some wanted to continue the war until Britain gave up Canada. Franklin had hated the war from the beginning. To those who wanted to see the war continue, he wrote: "May we never see another war! For in my opinion there never was a good war or a bad peace."

Franklin's will prevailed, and the peace treaty was signed in September 1783. Franklin remained in Europe for another two years as America's first ambassador to France. Finally in 1785, at the age of seventy-nine, Congress permitted him to come home. Thomas Jefferson, who took his place as ambassador, said: "I am not replacing Franklin. No one could do that. I am only his successor."

The new United States never welcomed a man home as wildly as they did their hero, Benjamin Franklin. Thousands of Philadelphians lined the wharf at Market Street. There were sounds of cheering and

OVERLEAF: *Conference of the Treaty
of Peace with England*
By Benjamin West
HENRY FRANCIS DU PONT WINTERTHUR MUSEUM

cannon fire as the ship approached the dock. Waiting with the crowd were Franklin's daughter, Sally, and his eight grandchildren. Now in constant pain from the gout, Franklin had to be helped off the ship. He was tired and could do nothing more than shake a few hands and go home.

Franklin tried to spend his last few years quietly reading and working in his laboratory. He was able to do this for two years. He read, continued his writing, and designed a fan that was powered by pushing a foot pedal. But in May 1787 the new United States of America held a convention for the purpose of drafting a new Constitution. At eighty-one Franklin was the oldest delegate at the convention.

Most of Franklin's early suggestions were rejected by the convention. One of his ideas was to divide the executive branch into three ministers rather than a single president. Franklin was reluctant to make new proposals after his early ones were turned down. He showed up at all the meetings but merely sat and listened. Sometimes he dozed off, and younger delegates complained about his snoring.

The major problem facing the convention was how the states should be represented in the national assembly. The larger states, such as New York and Virginia, wanted to be represented by population alone. The smaller states wanted all states to be equal in the assembly. Franklin provided a compromise. He backed a plan that would set up two houses: one, the Senate, in which each state would have two members, and two, the House of Representatives, which would have one member for each 40,-000 inhabitants. The compromise plan was approved, and the United States government is still structured in this way.

In September 1787 the new Constitution was signed. Franklin, one of the signers, was the only one of the founding fathers whose name appears on all of the four documents that turned the British colonies into an independent nation. His signature is on the Declaration of Independence, the treaty with France, the peace treaty with England, and on the Constitution.

After the Constitution was ratified, Franklin retired completely from public life. He lived long enough to see a stable government established in the United States, with George Washington at its head. Just before he died, he wrote Washington: "For my own personal ease I should have died two years ago; but, though those years have been spent in excruciating pain, I am pleased that I have lived them, since they have brought me to see our present situation."

Franklin died on April 17, 1790, when he was eighty-four. He was buried beside his wife, Deborah, in Philadelphia. Twenty thousand people marched behind his body to the grave. Church bells tolled, and men and women all over the United States wept.

Franklin directed in his will that a very simple inscription be written over his grave. His inscription reads: "Benjamin and Deborah Franklin, 1790." But more than sixty years earlier, when he was only twenty-three, the young printer wrote a different epitaph. It is strange that a twenty-three-year-old should think about the writing on his gravestone. Young Ben must have been in a very melancholy mood back in 1728 when he thought of death and wrote:

THE BODY

OF

BENJAMIN FRANKLIN

PRINTER

(LIKE THE COVER OF AN OLD BOOK,

ITS CONTENTS TORN OUT,

AND STRIPT OF ITS LETTERING AND GILDING),

LIES HERE, FOOD FOR WORMS.

BUT THE WORK SHALL NOT BE LOST,

FOR IT WILL (AS HE BELIEVED) APPEAR ONCE MORE,

IN A NEW AND MORE ELEGANT EDITION

REVISED AND CORRECTED

BY

THE AUTHOR

Index

PRINTED IN U.S.A.

REMARKS

Upon the Navigation from

NEWFOUNDLAND TO NEW-YORK,

In order to avoid the

GULPH STREAM

*On one hand, and on the other the SHOALS that lie to the Southward of
Nantucket and of St. George's Banks.*

AFTER you have paſſed the Banks of Newfoundland in about
the 44th degree of latitude, you will meet with nothing, till
you draw near the Iſle of Sables, which we commonly paſs in latitude 43. Southward of this iſle, the current is found to extend
itſelf as far North as 41° 20′ or 30′, then it turns towards the E.
S. E. or S. E. ¼ E.

Having paſſed the Iſle of Sables, ſhape your courſe for the St.
George's Banks, ſo as to paſs them in about latitude 40°, becauſe
the current ſouthward of thoſe banks reaches as far North as 39°.
The ſhoals of thoſe banks lie in 41° 35′.

After having paſſed St. George's Banks, you muſt, to clear Nantucket, form your courſe ſo as to paſs between the latitudes 38° 30′
and 40° 45′.

The moſt ſouthern part of the ſhoals of Nantucket lie in about
40° 45′. The northern part of the current directly to the ſouth of
Nantucket is felt in about latitude 38° 30′.

By obſerving theſe directions and keeping between the ſtream
and the ſhoals, the paſſage from the Banks of Newfoundland to
New-York, Delaware, or Virginia, may be conſiderably ſhorten-
ed; for ſo you will have the advantage of the eddy current, which
moves contrary to the Gulph Stream. Whereas if to avoid the
ſhoals you keep too far to the ſouthward, and get into that ſtream,
you will be retarded by it at the rate of 60 or 70 miles a day.

The Nantucket whale-men being extremely well acquainted with
the Gulph Stream, its courſe, ſtrength and extent, by their con-
ſtant practice of whaling on the edges of it, from their iſland quite
down to the Bahamas, this draft of that ſtream was obtained from
one of them, Capt. Folger, and cauſed to be engraved on the old
chart in London, for the benefit of navigators, by

B. FRANKLIN.

Note, The Nantucket captains who are acquainted with this
ſtream, make their voyages from England to Boſton in as
ſhort a time generally as others take in going from Boſton
to England, viz. from 20 to 30 days.

A ſtranger may know when he is in the Gulph Stream, by
the warmth of the water, which is much greater than that
of the water on each ſide of it. If then he is bound to the
weſtward, he ſhould croſs the ſtream to get out of it as ſoon
as poſſible.

B. F.